I Live a SAWDNESS

Life

Janice Michaelis

To order additional copies of this book, contact:
Xlibris
1-888-795-4274
www.Xlibris.com
Orders@Xlibris.com

To my loving fiancé, Amit, for always pushing me to be the best that I can be and for all your love and support.

Table of Contents

I Live a SAWDNESS Life

Delight

Petals pale, edges white,
brushed on cheek, scent quite nice.
Goosebumps perk, a smile slight.
Serotonin flows, a sensory delight.

Spring

Morning mists soak the grass.
Flowers bloom, bees on staff.
Leaves of green, bright-blue sky.
Puffy clouds floating by.
Bushy-tailed squirrels, flowering trees,
Perky sun, flowing breeze.

Blanket

Luxurious softness, comfy calm,
warm embrace, seven feet long.
Silver sheen, smooth, soft fleece,
Light turned out, solitary peace.

Rainbow

Red, yellow, orange, green, blue, and purple.
My favorite color is a rainbow.

Self-Improvement

Cells spark dull,
Silence of speech,
Eager to learn,
Needing that breach.
Hitting the books,
No time to spare,
Grammar improving,
I'm getting there.
Cells sparking,
rapid pace,
words keep flowing,
right in place.
No stone unturned,
I applied myself,
My brain at full function
And confidence top shelf.

Post-it

Pastel-yellow paper
crushed beneath my grasp,
creases define you
with the sound of rasp.
Pastel-yellow paper,
what to do with you?
Flicked you with my finger.
Into the trash you flew.

Transcending

I deny you, yet you remain,
Staining my aura with no refrain.
In my thoughts, in my dreams,
Nothing is quite what it seems.
Fire, water, earth, and wind,
Give me the strength to transcend.
Free from fear but not from harm,
Mental clarity has its charm.

Trauma

Hazy gaze through the night,
In a dimly lit room, no switch in sight.
The moon is out and peering through
A blinded window I once knew.
Silence lingers in the void
Of my old bedroom I destroyed.
A distant memory of the past,
Placing my fragile heart in a pace so face.
How did this come to be, a trail of
heartbreak reminding me?
Deception, perversion, and humility to name a few.
In some way I wish I never knew
That all that trauma came from you.

Freedom

Tickity tock, tickity tock,
Racing against time, I hate that clock.
I feel cheated. I feel rushed.
Clinkity, clankity, I'm going nuts.
I picked it up, then threw it with a frown.
My eyes ease up as I calm down.
Room is peaceful, silence of sound,
taking a moment as I lay on the ground.
Heart at ease, the moment has passed,
Put on my sneakers, adventure at last.

Landscape

Acrylic paint on my brush,
Took my time, no need to rush.
White, puffy clouds floating by
and resting on mountaintops way up high.
Down below a valley green,
a river running through with a sunny sheen.

Janice Nicholson

A Typical Day

Dirty feet on my table.

I want to scold you,

But I'm not able.

I'm a professional, and you're my client.

You know better, but you're defiant.

In a heater await two towels.

If I don't apply them, it will hurt my bowels.

In a room dim and calm,

I stand there watching the clock tick on.

An hour over, not much relief,

Got to prepare for the brief debrief.

On to the next, four more to go.

My tummy is hungry. Come on, let's go.

End of shift, I'm ready to know

How many clients left me dough.

Stop the Cycle

Mistake, mistake, mistake,

Please cut me a break.

I'm overstressed and making a mess.

I need this addressed.

Chaos is what I'm about.

How can I sort it out?

I'm here or there. I'm everywhere.

It gives the impression that I don't care.

Directed anger right at me,

Please, please hear my plea.

I'm in a rut, so out of luck.

I feel this journey is going to suck.

Taking a Ride

I rode my bike on a busy sidewalk.
The sidewalk is by the bay, visually
nice but smelly and polluted.
I coast down a mighty hill.
The pace is fast and quite a thrill.
The wind pounds my face in a passive hurry,
Drying my sweat, cooling my temperature.
The bike seat presses uncomfortably on my bum.
I'm pedaling faster to make it home
Before my bum becomes painfully numb.

Rain

Droplets fall upon my face.
The warmth of them all,
A liquid embrace.

Tattoo

My eyes slam shut, and I breathe real deep,
Vibration and buzzing trying hard not to leap.
Blood and ink gather there.
With every stride there is a tear.
Filling the void of my choice of design
Runs right up my bony spine.
Splashes of blue, purple, and green,
The artist depicts a beautiful, colorful scene.

Florida

Winter brings an arctic chill.
Doesn't snow, never will.
A chilly breeze and tall palm trees
Will never see a winter freeze.

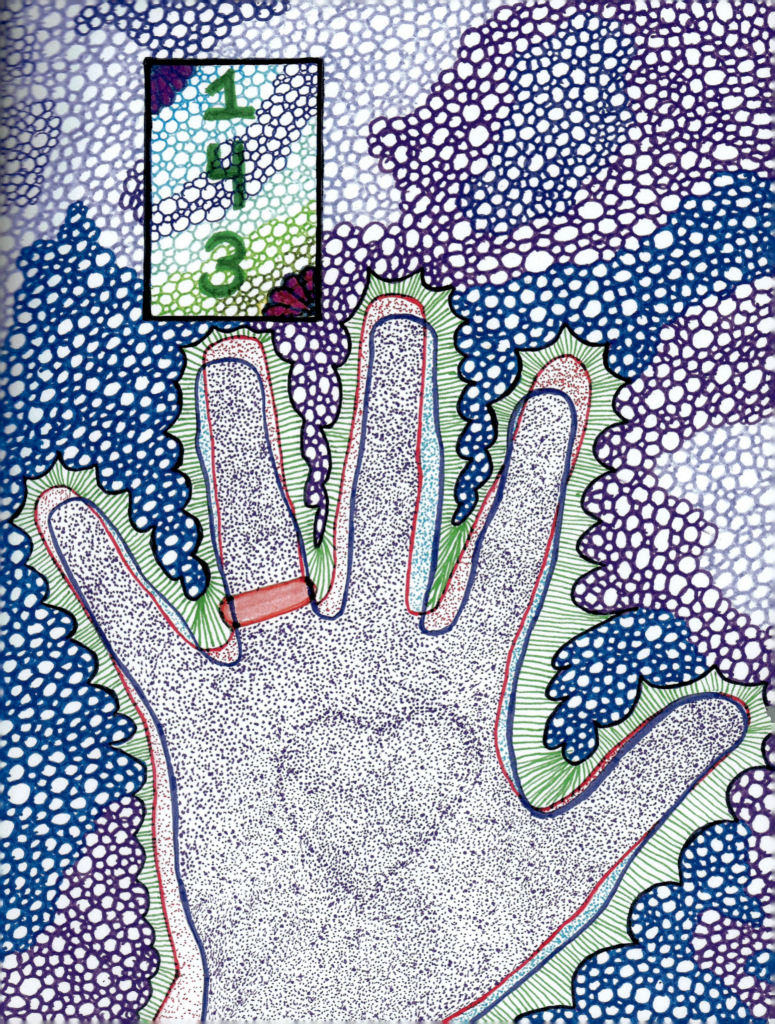

Amit

Hold my hand till I sleep.
It's better than counting sheep.
You secure me with your presence.
Even in my dreams I take comfort in your essence.

Foodie Problems

Yo-yo dieting every year,
What is the issue? It's not clear.
A balanced diet I applied,
Yet my waist size can't decide.
Up, down, through the wringer,
If this keeps up, I'll have to use my Singer.

A Simple Greeting

A man sits on a lonely bench at a bus stop
And watches busy feet as they walk by.
Hiding under his hat and sitting quietly,
He comes off as shy.
A woman took a seat next to him.
She politely says hello.
He looks over at her and nods his head,
Gets up, and says, "I got to go."

Dancing Outside

Beep boop on my stoop,
Bopping around like I gotta poop.
Having fun, throwing waves,
Yep, yep, feeling brave.

My Favorite Shoes

I love my shoes, so sporty yet casual.
I wear them with jeans and with shorts.
I wear them at work and during sports.
I was drawn to them when I saw them,
blue leather with four stripes of white.
I tried them on, and they felt right.
I kept them on as I paid for them
and wore them out.
I will wear them
until I cannot wear them anymore.

Encounter

Tiny owl in the street,
How lucky it is for us to meet.
I'm in my car. You're in the road.
I stopped in time as you strode
giving you time to cross.

A Poem for Him

You make me smile.
You make me laugh.
You're a lion, and I'm a giraffe.
You are fierce, and you are strong.
You serenade me with your song.
Tall and graceful I stand there,
Fluttering heart, loving stare.
Ten years strong we've been together,
Unlikely beasts living happily forever.

Thinking

Sitting at my kitchen island,
listening to my favorite band,
thinking about writing poetry,
twirling my hair in my hand.

While You're Sleeping

In the night I miss you.
I reach over and try to kiss you.
You're breathing deep
and counting sheep
while I'm over here losing sleep
reaching over for you.

Misha

His blue doe eyes are filled with joy.
His love for life you can't destroy.
He talks with a playful smirk,
showing his confidence in his works.
His heart is filled with love and kindness.
I aspire to be of the likeness.
He's my idol, my hero, my guru too.
He inspires me to be a better person
through and through.

Spontaneous

Your car is rockin'
and your persona is too.
Let's go for a ride and find something to do.
We find a quiet carnival
in a rural town.
We spot a grand ol' elephant
carrying a goofy clown.
Fireworks bursting out of nowhere,
what an amazing sight.
Hunger approaches. Let's go grab a bite.

Into the Wilderness

I find myself needing time away from my busy life—an escape to solitude, fresh air, and peace. I reach my destination and feel a cascading calm fall over me. I'm in my happy place, a place full of peace, serenity, and beauty. I'm surrounded by miles of trees decorating the massive forest-green mountains. I'm amazed by how many varieties of trees there are here. Most of the trees are smothered with vines with heart-shaped leaves. It's noon now, but the trees provide me shade. I feel the cool breeze and take a moment to enjoy this wonderful gift that the earth has given to me. There is a porch swing placed between two trees in the front yard. I take a seat and begin to swing back and forth. I slowly take in a few slow, deep breaths and gently allow my eyes to close. My senses seem to heighten, and now I can focus on the sounds of nature with more of a grounded, personal experience.

A breeze rushes past my ears and makes wind-tunnel noises. Flowing water in a creek trying to make its way downstream over smooth stones makes a soothing melody. Cicadas rattle a song—a competition to be the loudest, I presume. A distant rumble quakes the sky as warm droplets faintly patter upon the crisp leaves. The rain quickly crashes to the ground in an ascending clatter. The storm has arrived and reached its aggression, but I still sit there with my eyes closed on the porch swing. I sit there allowing the rain to cleanse the woes that city life dumped on me. I sit there feeling more alive than I've ever been, more grounded, more self-aware. I pray for the rain to continue for just a moment more, not wanting the purifying droplets to miss a single negative stain within me.

The rain has ceased, the sun peers through the clouds, and the birds sing their songs once more. I slowly open my eyes, for they sense the sun. I take a few slow deep breaths, stand up, and grin. I feel reborn. Here I go, back out into the world, ready to take on whatever comes next.

Printed in the United States
By Bookmasters